Content

Foreword: Setting the scene.

1: Formation of Kinghorn Loch.   1

2: Pre-historic and Early times.   3

3: Medieval Times – Evidence of the first mill at Craigencalt.   6

4: The First Watermill   9

5: The Leslie family buys the lands of Craigencalt.   11

6: Lands of Craigencalt pass to Raith Estate.   14

7: The Young Family Connection - A New Watermill.   21

8: The Robert Philp Educational Trust takes ownership.   31

9: Water Supply for Kinghorn   44

10: Changing Times   45

11: Banchory and Drinkbetween Farms   49

12: Kinghorn and Kinghorn Loch   53

References   55

Acknowledgments and postscript.   58

Foreword: Setting the scene.

For such a tiny hamlet, Craigencalt has a long and fascinating history and much of the heritage is still there to see.

Kinghorn Loch, an attractive and useful natural feature has served the peoples of the area throughout its whole existence. It was an unusual but fortunate act of nature that caused the surroundings to be so attractive, with the formation of Kinghorn Loch as a 'kettle hole lake' at the end of the last glaciation of the present Ice Age. The loch will have been formed sometime between 13,000 and 11,000 years ago; the date is uncertain as there was a re-advance of the ice during this time. This was followed by a rapid warming of the climate. A rocky tundra with numerous lochans and the scattering of birch, alder and possibly pine woodland will have greeted the first hunter-gatherer stone age groups as they migrated across the land bridge from Europe into Britain. Slowly, nature and farmers will have cleared and cultivated the land but even in the nineteenth century much drainage work was still needed. From medieval times, its attractiveness as a site of a productive mill close to the coastal transport routes and as a water supply for Kinghorn has brought colourful and powerful landowners and philanthropists onto the scene, in partnership and in disagreement. Today the many visitors to Craigencalt and Kinghorn Loch can enjoy the countryside and water sports and can learn about all the twists and turns of these colourful people.

Craigencalt Farm showing development of the mill buildings and farm house.

? Corn mill extant at or before 1583 - position unknown.

1. Corn mill built well before 1682, used until around 1790.

2. Threshing mill built around 1790, used until around 1860.

3. Craigencalt Farmhouse, built 1891.

1: Formation of Kinghorn Loch.

In the beginning there was only ice - for two and a half million years with hundreds of metres of ice over Kinghorn at its greatest thickness. This last glacial period of the present Ice Age came to an end only around 11,000 years ago, as we entered an inter-glacial period.

Glaciers of the central Scotland ice sheet grind towards the North Sea ice sheet.

As the front of the central Scotland ice sheet receded past Kinghorn a huge calf of ice broke away and was buried in moraine (rock and clay). When this huge block melted it left a hole in the landscape which became Kinghorn Loch. Such lochs are usually round and deep and are referred to as 'Kettle Hole' lakes. They are quite unusual. The landscape will have been rocky tundra with characteristic sharp rocky knolls with bog and lochans between. Soon, sparse birch and alder woodland followed, with pine and ultimately oak forest coming in.

As the weight of ice was removed from the land, the land rebounded and continues to do so today. Initially the sea level rose by 45m through ice melt but then fell back as land rose. Britain was connected to Europe until around 8,500 years ago when the land bridge to Britain finally vanished beneath the sea. This will have been fertile land and hunter-gatherers will have already moved north into Scotland, moving further northwards with the retreating ice.

The tundra would have shown a landscape quite different from today.

Tundra photographs courtesy of Michael Kirsh

Kinghorn Loch.

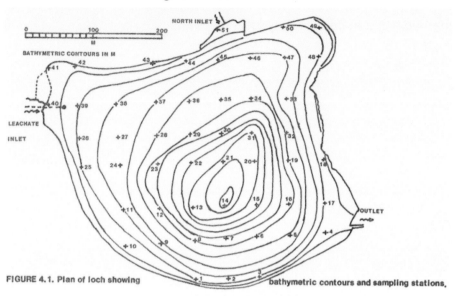

FIGURE 4.1. Plan of loch showing bathymetric contours and sampling stations.

Cross-section of Kinghorn Loch

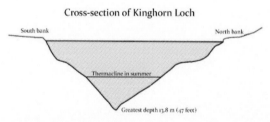

Kinghorn Loch is a roughly circular loch with a diameter of approximately 380 m. It is relatively deep, being 13.8 m at its greatest depth. A thermacline develops over the summer when upper waters can typically be 13-18°C while that below the thermacline can be 4°C. The thermacline may turn over in autumn and mixing occurs. The only significant inflow to the loch is the burn at Craigencalt Farm and residence time for water is typically eight months. Water in the burn is primarily derived from the Banchory Burn, the burn being diverted as a mill lade across the fields in the sixteenth or seventeenth century.

Reference: 'Impact of a long-term caustic discharge from Red Mud disposal on a freshwater lake', R.A.Edwards, PhD Thesis, University of Edinburgh (1985)

2

2: Pre-historic and Early times.

It is not by accident that people decide to live where they do, and the area around Kinghorn Loch has been an excellent place for habitation since the retreat of the last glaciers, when humans came and settled in Scotland. The basic requirements for living were in abundance here, a plentiful supply of fresh water with running springs to avoid stagnation, a good terrain, soil to grow some crops and woodland for hunting and providing fuel. This place had easy access to the coast for fishing and trading and its elevated position provided good look out points and expansive views across the Firth of Forth and inland.

Evidence of the first Mesolithic people to settle here in the Caledonian forests as the glaciers receded, has been uncovered around the Firth of Forth. In November 2001, a small seasonal encampment was found at Crammond in Edinburgh, at the mouth of the River Almond. More recently, in November 2012 it was reported in The Scotsman [1] that, while builders were preparing the ground for the new Forth Road Bridge (Queensferry Crossing), evidence was discovered of a dwelling. The site is at Echline, near South Queensferry, and has been dated to around 10,000 years ago. The discovery comprises a large oval pit 7 metres in length which would have been a dwelling house, perhaps for one or more families. There is evidence of post holes, supported walls and a turf roof. Inside there were several hearths where charred shells and hazel

© Transport Scotland/Headland Archaeology

nut kernels were found, suggesting that diet was good and varied. More than 1,000 flint artefacts were uncovered including several flint arrowheads. It is evident that the Echline community lived quite comfortably.

The Picts were the first people to settle in the north and east of Scotland. We are still learning much about them through archaeological discoveries. They had farming and fishing skills and their lasting communication was by means of pictures and symbols carved on rocks. Further exciting evidence has been uncovered of Pictish people living in the vicinity of Kinghorn Loch. In July 2003, the Scotsman [2] reported that two amateur archaeologists, Colin Kilgour and Jock Moyes from Burntisland had discovered cup and ring and spiral design markings on boulders on the Binn Hill above Burntisland, only some 5 km from Kinghorn Loch. Historic Scotland confirmed that these were Neolithic and about 4,000 years old. This

Carving on The Binn © Ian Kilgour

find is about 3,000 years older than the well known Pictish carvings at Wemyss caves, further along the Fife coast. Although we do not have archaeological evidence that Pictish people settled at Kinghorn Loch itself, it is perfectly possible that they did.

In my research there are various references to an early (post-Roman) battle that reportedly took place near Kinghorn between a combined force of Picts, Scots and Britons and an invading force of Angles who arrived in the Forth Estuary by boat. Physical evidence for such an encounter has never been established. However, in the year 596AD there is an account of the Battle of Raith or Catraeth (Cat being the Irish and Gaelic name for a battle) which may have taken place immediately to the west of Kirkcaldy. The battle was described in a poem by a Welsh bard called Hanerurin who was present at the fighting. The invaders were Angles and King Aidan (King of the Scots of Dalriada, crowned by Saint Columba at Iona) and his nobles were defending. The fighting went on for over a week and the invaders eventually retreated but King Aidan suffered heavy losses. In The Celtic Review VII published in 1911 [3] Mr E B W Nicholson, a Bodleian librarian in Oxford, wrote that a charge of 300 men took place down Raith hill by the west of the mill dam and along to the Tiel Burn. However there are several claims for the battle's location in various places throughout Britain.

There is also a description of the Battle of Kinghorn around 900AD recorded in an article in the Dundee Courier in May 1875 [4]. The Battle occurred between Viking kings, King Duncan I of Scotland and King

Canute of England. Canute sailed up the Forthwith his fleet. This battle is reported to have been fought on high ground above Kinghorn, with Macbeth and Macduff defending the territory. The slain chieftains were reportedly taken to Inchcolm for burial. A small chapel was erected in memory of the battle and there is indeed a small ruined chapel of unknown date, in a field at Glassmount, shown on

Standing Stones at Glassmount

Ordnance Survey maps. According to the newspaper article, centuries later, two obelisk stones were erected in a field at Glassmount to record the battle, and these can be seen from the Standing Stanes Road. In 1934 the two obelisks were given ancient monument status [5]. No clear evidence for the battle has ever been found and there appears to be no definite source for the story, but it makes good reading.

3: Medieval Times – Evidence of the first mill at Craigencalt.

What is in a name? Often a name relates to the features or appearance of a place and this is likely to be the reason for the Pictish variants of Kirncat, Craigynkat or Craigencat. The rocky outcrops in the land are certainly a prominent feature in the surrounding area, and the name may hold a simple explanation as the "gorge of the wild cats" or another translation is possibly "crag of the mad man". The spelling of Craigencalt has taken many forms over the centuries, and is enough to send a computer into spell check frenzy. The first mention of Cragyncat in the constabulary of Kinghorn came in 1358 in the Place Names of Fife. Just ten years later, in 1368 it was recorded in the Register of the Great Seal when David II parcelled out land to overlords in Scotland [6]. This was a way of him raising funds to pay a ransom to the English King in return for his freedom and his return to Scotland after eleven long years of incarceration. So, in 1368, Sir John Abernethy, in the parish of Kinghorn was granted lands of Balwearie, Boglily and Cragnkat.

By 1430 the barony of Balmuto, and lands in the constabulary of Kinghorn had passed to the Boswell family who had Norman ancestry dating back to 1066 when they fought with William the Conqueror at the Battle of Hastings. Roger de Boswell was the first of the family to settle in Fife when he married Mariota, the heiress to half of the Barony of Auchterderran. Roger's great grandson Sir John Boswell was the first of Balmuto and Balgeddie and his son, David de Boswylll of Cragyngate had a ruling made in his favour for the right of patronage in the parish of Auchterderran in 1444 [7]. It was through marriage and inheritance that, in the Register of the Great Seal in 1458 [8], Sir David Boswell of Balmuto owned lands at Glassmount, Craigincalt, Boglily and Dundonald. This Sir David Boswell also had a son called David of Balmuto, born 1498 and died 1582.

In 1583 we first hear of a working mill at Craigencalt, with John Boswell receiving rents from land at Craigencat, Damhead and the mill, mill-lands and acres at Craigencalt [9]. The same year an Instrument of Sasine [10] made in favour of *"James Bosuall, son of John Bosuall of Balmowto and Issobella Sandelandis, his spouse, infefting him in an annual rent of 8 bolls of wheat, 16 bolls of barley and 16 bolls of oatmeal furth of the town and land of Craigincat, Damheid and the mill, mill-lands and acres of Craigincat, in the parish of Kingorne Eister and sheriffdom of Fife; on precept of sasine in charter"*, dated 4 May 1583 by John Boswell. The mention of Damhead indicates that a mill pond already existed there and so the lade must have been dug from South Glassmount to the mill pond - a considerable venture. Thus the mill at Craigencalt may well have existed long before 1583.

At this time Craigencalt was in a favourable position as the Great North Road from the ferry terminals at Kinghorn, and to a lesser extent Burntisland met at the head of the loch at Gallowhill. It proceeded along the farm track at the head of the loch and across the north of Cow Hill to the track passing Damhead, through Banchory and Drinkbetween to Kirkcaldy and on to the Tay ferry for Dundee. This route, some of which still exists as a farm track, was replaced around 1793 by the present Kirkcaldy Road along the south bank of Kinghorn Loch. There was some concern in Kinghorn about the route taken and disruption caused[163,164,165].

Balmuto Castle

Piteadie Castle

7

The Boswell family has a long association with the local area and the family castle at Balmuto has been restored in recent times. The family found favour with James IV of Scotland, and some died with him at Flodden; they continued to be close to the monarchy. In 1547, David Boswell was killed at the Battle of Pinkie [10]. The family supported Charles I during the Civil War. In the 17th century another David Boswell had work done on Piteadie Castle, which still stands as a ruin viewed from the Jawbane Road to Kirkcaldy.

James Stuart of Dunearn
(1775-1849)

Perhaps the most famous story is that of Alexander Boswell who took part in one of the last duels in Fife. The duel took place on 26th March 1822 in a field at Balbarton Farm [12]. The dispute was over something really trivial, a poem that appeared in a Glasgow gazette which suggested James Stuart of Dunearn was a coward. When James Stuart found out who had written the piece, he asked Boswell to apologise. It was only after Alexander Boswell refused that the duel took place. The two met in a field near Balbarton at dawn. Alexander Boswell was fatally wounded and died at Balmuto Castle a few days later. Sadly, he was known as a talented writer who may have gone on to produce great works had he lived. Stuart faced trial but was found not guilty as he had asked for an apology [13].

4: The First Watermill

We do not know when the first water mill was constructed at Craigencalt but it would have been identified as a good site, with a gorge and natural surrounding springs to feed into it. Watermills were a developing feature from Roman times and even possibly Pictish times before then. The first mills were often built of wood but, if stone was readily available, then it was used in mills as the buildings needed to be robust against vibration from the water-wheel and mill stones turning. There was also damaging dampness from water seeping through walls, so repairs were regularly required [14]. There was plenty of stone available at Craigencalt. The usual layout of a corn mill was that the lower floor was used for grinding and grain store, while the upper floor was used for the cleaning of the grain and floor storage.

The Boswell family owned the mill In 1583, but we do not know what it looked like or its exact location. We do know that during the 16th and 17th century a lot of improvements were made to the efficiency of mills. In 1583 there is mention of "Damheid" [9,10] and seventeenth century maps also show that a lade channel had been dug from the Banchory Burn through to Damheid Park, where a mill pond had been created. This construction would have incurred a great deal of manual labour and effort, so must have been well worth while. The first mill may have been at Damhead, or lower down, towards the loch at Craigencalt. There is no way of knowing exactly where the very first mill was sited.

There is mention of a "Damheid Mill" in references but it is unlikely that the mill would have been at Damhead as there may have been insufficient drop for a wheel to operate. Damhead was, however on the Great North Road from the ferries at Kinghorn and Burntisland to Dundee which would have given it advantage. It is more likely to have been within or below the gorge closer to the loch, where the drop for the wheel was greater. For the second option it appears that the natural stream channel would be utilised to carry water from the pond to the mill near the lochside. The mill was definitely situated at the lochside well before 1682. The layout of the water supply to the mill is shown in the later map of 1757 [15]. It is possible that the existing, old mill building at the lochside dates from around 1583, but there is no confirmation of a mill at this location before 1682 [16] although by that date it was evidently old and in need of substantial repairs.

On 1st May 1600 the Instrument of Sasine in favour of David Boswell (4th son of John Boswell) gave him an annual rent of 400 merks from the lands of Craigigate (Craigencalt) [17]. In November 1611 Sir John Boswell sold the land of Craigencat to his brothers and the land was split in two, giving James Boswell the northern half and David southern half for 56000 merks [18]. The mill may have been productive as both a corn and malting mill, as in 1628, in a contract of Wadset, Simon and Robert Chrystie, brothers and maltmen of the burgess of Kinghorn were renting 18 acres of land at Craigencalt [19]. This is the first hint that the mill at Craigencalt may have been used for preparing barley for brewing. Then, in 1642, Craigincat Mill and lands were sold by David Boswell to Alexander Leslie, first Earl of Leven [11]. Both the Gordon map of 1642 and the Blaeu map of 1654 show the mill and the loch (referred to as Craigncatt Lake.) which suggests the mill was of significant importance.

Typical mill of this era. Similar to the old mill building.

Blaeu Atlas of Scotland 1654 showing a mill at Kinghorn Loch

10

5: The Leslie family buys the lands of Craigencalt.

Alexander Leslie, the first Earl of Leven, acquired the lands and Barony of Balgonie, Treaton Mire and lands of Craigencalt from the Boswell brothers [11] in July 1642. After his death, his widow Margaret Leslie retained a keen interest in the lands of Craigencalt.

Alexander Leslie, the first Earl of Leven was a renowned military campaigner who gained a distinguished reputation in war. He managed to retain his respectability during the difficult times of Civil War between Charles I and Cromwell's troops. He was a respected negotiator who only took up arms when all else failed. Towards the end of his career he invested his capital in Scotland and purchased land in Fife, which included the lands and Barony of Balgony, Treaton Mire and lands at Craigincat. He was married to Margaret Leslie with whom he had two children, Alexander born in 1637 and Catherine in 1638. Margaret, Lady Balgonie was a regular visitor to the local area and on a fine day, it was said that she liked to sit out at a place overlooking the Firth of Forth and Pettycur Harbour. This place gained the name "Lady Balgonie's seat".

Alexander Leslie, first Earl of Leven

After the death of Alexander Leslie, Margaret went on to marry Francis Scott, second Earl of Buccleuch, and when he also died she married David Wemyss, second Earl of Wemyss and had a further four children through these marriages. She died in 1688 a very rich lady.

Margaret Leslie, Lady Balgony, Doweger Countess of Wemyss

In 1660 John Wardlaw of Abden was renting Craigencalt from the Leslie family [21].

There is an excellent document [16] written on the order of Margaret Leslie, as Dowager Countess of Wemyss. It is a detailed audit of the mill at Craigencalt. It was compiled for her by Robert Bratston, the tacksman (collector of dues) of the Barony of Craigincalt and William Malcolm of Kirkcaldy. The account itemised a survey of repairs needed at Craigincalt mill and the surrounding buildings and was dated 6th October 1682. It is clear that the mill is quite old and in need of a lot of work. It is not only a wonderful insight into the structure and building at Craigencalt but even names the folk who lived there at that time.

It is a long account and to precis the findings: *"They find that the Mill House in Craigincalt is weak both in couples, timber and walls, and some of the couples broken and needing repair. The roof is good and the place is watertight. The barn walls and roof are sufficient but it is not watertight and the east wall needs pinning. The south barn had seven beams bought for the roof six years previously but they were never put in. The stable and south byre is sufficient but the east byre needs a lot of repair.*

Craigincalt Mill site house and stable is possessed by James Lightoun, although these buildings are sufficient, the barn and byres are near to the point of falling in. The water wall of the over mill is very weak and the water wheel requires some attention

There are two buildings at the west and east side of Damheid, situated by the mill pond. Andrew Muir lived at west side of Damheid and the pantiles and rigging are broken at his house. Also the couple of the barn is broken and the barn needs a new door. A site house possessed by Alexander Watson is described as in a ruinous state and needing great repair. John Lightoun lives on the east side of the Damhead. The house is sufficient except that the thatching needs some tending and in the barn there are two couples and pans broken".

The document interestingly refers to the stable and barn of Rodinbraes which is possessed by Johnnie Bonar. The site house needs couples mended to save the roof and lathing. Why Rodanbraes is included is unclear, perhaps this was linked to Craigencalt Mill in some way.

At the end of the report, it states that the repairs were carried out and these are described. There are two things that we may conclude from this detailed insight into the running of Craigencalt Mill. The one is that the mill and associated buildings had been in operation and perhaps neglected for a long time before 1682, so needed much attention. Repairs were seen as necessary to return to good condition as a growing business of some importance.

The other observation of prime importance is the tying up of the verbal description of the mill in 1682 and the Raith Estate map of 1757 [15] which clearly, and apparently accurately, shows the layout of the buildings. It is clear that both sources describe the same buildings and corroborate each other in detail.

The mill building that was extant in 1682 is now colloquially referred to as 'The Hermitage'.

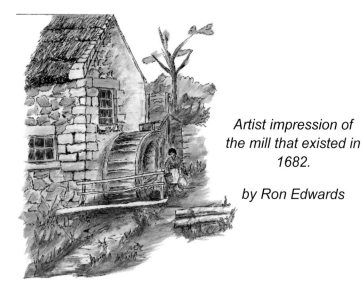

Artist impression of the mill that existed in 1682.

by Ron Edwards

6: Lands of Craigencalt pass to Raith Estate.

Catherine Leslie, Margaret's daughter, married George Melville, first Earl of Melville and Balgonie; Raith and Craigencalt became part of their Estate [28]. George suppressed the Covenentors, helped William of Orange to the throne and was made Secretary of State for Scotland and Keeper of the Privy seal. On George's death in 1707, Raith, including the lands of Craigencalt were sold to Robert Ferguson, [28.] an upwardly mobile man who was born into a wealthy, established family in Inverkeithing, who were part of Clan McFarlane [28]. Robert was born in 1690 in Inverkeithing, the son of James Ferguson, Baillie of Inverkeithing and Agnes Stewart. He went to live in his uncle's house in London where he did well for himself. He spent most of his life in London [22] where, in 1725, he married Mary Townsend, the daughter of Joseph Townsend, a merchant in London. They had no children. In 1738 he became Sheriff of London; he was successful and owned land and title in his native Fife. He died in 1781 at the age of 91. Latterly his nephew, William Berry, looked after his interests at Raith.

There are some mentions of tenancies at Craigencalt. In 1712 James Brown, tenant of Banchory, had tack for 9 years for lands at Craigencalt [23]. Also in 1715 there is tack for 19 years by the factor, Robert Birrell, to Patrick Heggie, shipmaster in Kinghorn, of lands at Yetland in Craigencalt. This gives a little insight that the land was rented for farming. In the Town Council minutes of 1730 there was a reference made to four mills that gave short measures to customers and the council officials warned that they would be visiting the owners of such mills to check up on them [24]. It may be that Craigencalt was one of them.

Robert Ferguson commissioned a detailed set of plans of all his estate lands in 1757. He was not alone in doing this around this time. Opportunities for better farming returns were happening and landowners wanted to explore their best options. New technology, like the use of lighter ploughs, was bringing about many changes in farming. New large water powered threshing machinery was being introduced. The desire was to improve the efficient cultivation of the land and maps were created to assist this. In the series of maps for Raith estate, surveyed by Thomas Winter, there is a detailed and accurate plan of the Barony of Craigencat [15]. A clarified image of this map is shown below.

The plan shows the original mill pond at Damheid Park and the old tofts nearby. There is the line of the stream to the mill, and the old mill with its barns and byres. It names some of the surrounding fields and these names still apply today. The new larger mill is not on this plan concluding

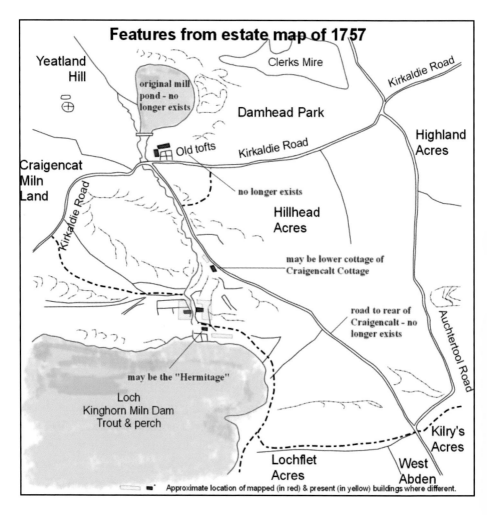

Features from estate map of 1757

Yeatland Hill

original mill pond - no longer exists

Clerks Mire

Kirkaldie Road

Damhead Park

Highland Acres

Old tofts

Kirkaldie Road

Craigencat Miln Land

Kirkaldie Road

no longer exists

Hillhead Acres

may be lower cottage of Craigencalt Cottage

road to rear of Craigencalt - no longer exists

Auchtertool Road

may be the "Hermitage"

Loch Kinghorn Miln Dam Trout & perch

Kilry's Acres

Lochflet Acres

West Abden

Approximate location of mapped (in red) & present (in yellow) buildings where different.

15

that a decision to build it and the new mill pond nearer the loch had not yet been made in 1757.

Because of damage to the map, it is difficult to see if the lower Craigencalt Cottage is present, but this is unlikely. The burn from Damhead to Craigencalt Mill is shown as a natural watercourse down through the gorge that later is altered to form the new Mill Pond, and there is no apparent connection between Damhead and Craigencalt, although there must have been a footpath at least. A road from the Kirkaldie Road (formerly Great North Road from the ferries to Dundee), going south east past Craigencalt travelled across the present fields directly to the bottom of Red Path Brae and although no longer existing, the route is still evident. There was no road through Craigencalt. Similarly the line of the Great North Road now only exists as the farm track from the Auchtertool public road at Charlies gate for 100 metres and then again from the west corner of Cowhill to Gallowhill, although the line of the remainder can still be followed. The Great North Road was replaced by the present road south of the loch around 1793[163,164,165].

Robert died on the 18th December 1781 in London at the age of 91 [25] and left his estate to his favoured nephew, William Berry the youngest son of David Berry and Agnes Ferguson. Robert Berry, William's older brother was left only £10,000 by his uncle together with an annuity of £300 [26]. Failure to leave the estate to the proper heir was a controversial thing to do and caused some acrimony within the family, as the published diary of Mary and Agnes Berry (Robert Berry's daughters) confirm [26]. The girls were also provided for and, although they resented losing their fortune, they appreciated that their father was not the most suitable heir. William Berry was born in London in October 1743 and held a close relationship with his uncle. When he inherited he was required to adopt the family name of Ferguson. In 1768 he married Jean Craufurd, who was from a wealthy family. They had two sons; Robert was born in 1769 and Ronald Craufurd Ferguson (who was to become a famous general [27]) was born in 1773, both born at Raith [28]. William took a great interest in the estate, developing Raith House into the main residence and converting Abbotshall House to gardens for the family and planning a park and pleasure grounds. Thomas White was employed to landscape the grounds and prepared a plan in 1783 which contained sunken fences, estate cottages, a reservoir, flower gardens and hot gardens including Beveridge Park. James Playfair's architectural scheme complimented the landscape, remodelling the interior of the house in 1785 [29]. Playfair's brother, John was persuaded by his brother to come and tutor William's sons Robert and Ronald, and imparted a love of geology for Robert which became a great interest throughout his life [29].

John Playfair (1748-1819) was an eminent scientist, professor of Natural Philosophy at the University of Edinburgh. He summarised the work of James Hutton in his book of 1802 *"Illustrations of the Huttonian Theory of the Earth"*. It was through this book that the realisation of the extreme age of the Earth first reached a wide audience [30].

John Playfair

We learn from the many published guides and diaries of the head gardener William Nicol, that follies were constructed at Torbain Tower, Lambswell, Raith Tower and the lake at Raith was formed [29].

It is highly probable that during his time as owner of Raith estate, the new and present mill building was constructed and the mill pond positioned where it is today, together with a mill cottage built near the dam. The cottage nearest the dam at Craigencalt Cottages is sometimes referred to as the Mill Cottage in later census records [31].

From 1790, William Ferguson had been intent on modernising his seat at Raith House and his farms and at some point he, and possibly Robert, were working with a new tenant at Craigencalt Mill, wealthy and influential William Young, to bring a new mill into use, a threshing mill rather than the old corn mill.

On 20th July 1790 a Bill of Suspension and Interdict was recorded for Kinghorn Town Council [32]. The representatives of the Council were the Provost, Andrew Hamilton and Kinghorn Burgh Tacksman for the mills,

William Balmain. They put forward the case that the Loch Burn, which was regulated by a sluice at the mouth of the loch and provided water for the mills in Kinghorn lacked water because the rivulet that runs into the loch at Craigencalt had been diverted. William Ferguson and his tenants, John Ewan and William Fair had taken it upon themselves to divert the natural curve of the rivulet, preventing it from reaching the loch and thus depriving the town of water. The ruling was in favour of the town as there was a right of the public of Kinghorn to the water in the loch. No reason for the diversion was given by William Ferguson in the correspondence. There were a number of entries to the Town Council Minutes on this subject[160,161,162] but no information on why it happened.

Around this time the new mill pond and mill construction works may have taken place. During the construction of the mill dam in the gorge it would have been an attractive idea to release the lade water coming from South Glassmount into the Banchory Burn (where once it had been diverted from, in the sixteenth or seventeenth century) and thus being able to construct the dam dry. The consequences were to upset Kinghorn which was always potentially short of water for its mills. This evidence may give a likely date for the construction of the new mill.

The First Statistical Accounts of Scotland in 1791 [33] gives some interesting factual information about Kinghorn and the surrounding countryside. It comments that names like Kingswood and Woodfield Park and other lands to the west of Kinghorn were once covered in dense woodland and would have been good hunting ground for nobility It says that most landowners did not reside in the area but let and sub-let land on 19 year leases. The land spread of Kinghorn farms was given as 3050 acres of arable and 340 not arable (mainly hilly ground covered with gorse or trees). On average there was 170 acres of wheat, 397 of barley, 212 of peas and beans which were sewn in drills, 749 of oats, 148 of potatoes, 110 of turnips, 328 of hay, 836 of pasture and 100 summer fallows but no flax. The land was mostly enclosed by hedge and ditch, called Galloway Dikes. The best arable land price was £31/acre and the best pasture £21..5/- shillings/acre. There were 250 horses reared locally, 70 were kept in the town for coal and general haulage and carriages. The cattle were short horned and the sheep mainly cheviot or black face crosses. There were 651 cows, 99 carts and 91 ploughs, each drawn by 2 horses. The country inhabitants were generally sober, industrious, charitable and skilful according to the account. In 1793 there were 3 flax spinning mills in Kinghorn; Kinghorn Mill, St Leonards and Nethergate but Craigencalt is not mentioned as ever being part of the flax milling. In the Gazette of Scotland in 1831, the population of Kinghorn is given as 2,579 with 146 families employed in agriculture.

Improvements in farming continued in the 19th century, with more land being brought into productive use through better drainage. The industrial revolution which was sweeping the country at this time, brought many innovations to agriculture.

William Ferguson died in 1810 and Robert, his eldest son, inherited the estate.

Robert was a well educated man and an eminent geologist. He was elected to Parliament in 1806 to represent Fifeshire [27] and in later years became Lord Lieutenant of Fife [28]. Whilst journeying in France, Robert was confined to house arrest by Napoleon, along with Thomas Bruce, Earl of Elgin (of Elgin Marbles fame) and his wife Mary. His relationship with eminent French scientists and the strings pulled from Britain eventually led to his release. He arrived back at Raith in October 1804. However, it seems he subsequently returned to France to escort Mary Elgin home when she in turn was released from house arrest in February 1805, for it was reports of Ferguson's presence on the boat to England that first alerted Lord Elgin to the love affair between Robert and Mary. He had them watched and intercepted many of their letters that were described by Elgin at the ensuing trial as "the most ridiculous medley of love and madness" that would "disgrace the worst novel of the last century" [34]. Robert's affair was public and Thomas Bruce divorced Mary and successfully sued Robert for £10,000, to compensate for his distress. Some say this money enabled him to bring the Elgin Marbles to Britain. Robert and Mary returned to live at

Monument to Robert Ferguson MP in Haddington

Ferguson decided to sell some of his farms to the newly formed Philp Trust in 1829. He was required to do this because of the big debts that he needed to settle. These were itemised in an Act of Parliament [35] that was required because he was not passing these lands to his estate on his death. His financial affairs were overseen in his last years by a trust, headed by Lord Rosslyn. On Robert's death, the family inheritance went to his brother Ronald Crauford Ferguson and the Munro Ferguson family remain at Raith today. The Philp Trust saw the investment in land and farming as a reliable way to get good returns in rent each year to support their Philp Schools.

7: The Young Family Connection - A New Watermill.

As the research has progressed, an important link between Craigencalt Mill and Grange Distillery in Burntisland (William Young & Co,) has been established. William Young and Sons, through William the father and then William (Jnr) and Robert, his sons, were important tenants of William and then Robert Ferguson at Craigencalt Mill and finally the Philp Trust; an association spanning fifty years and more.

Indeed, the first mention that the mill may have been used in the production of alcohol was in 1628. Two brothers, Simon and Robert Chrystie, maltmen, and burgesses of Kinghorn held a Contract of Wadset from James and David Boswell for 18 acres of land at Craigencalt [19]. We do know that it was a working mill for all of the seventeenth century and corn, barley and oats were all mentioned in rent at this time [36].

During the eighteenth century the industrial revolution saw power-driven machinery introduced on farms. Large, improved threshers came into use to relieve what was back-breaking and time-consuming work, but these machines required much more room to function, so larger mill buildings were constructed during this time. Water, using overshot wheels, like the one at Craigencalt, extracted the maximum power from small streams. Water mills were much cheaper to run than horse driven ones, and in Scotland such mills were common [46]. Often these watermills were kept going for threshing on the farm even after steam powered threshers were introduced, as low running costs made it worthwhile to keep the wheel in good running order [46].

It is easy to see how the mill at Craigencalt would be a convenient asset for the Young family moving to Burntisland in 1786. William Young brought his family to Burntisland, putting the family estate [37], farms and distillery [38] at Hattonburn, Orwell, Milnathort up for sale. However the estate was eventually sequestrated to pay off debts of £14,772 with an eventual payout of 10/- in the pound [39,40]. He soon established the Grange Distillery which had previously been a brewery. William will have begun making new business contacts and may well have discussed a new threshing mill with William Ferguson. William (Jnr) and later Robert took over the management of the distillery and it prospered, a new distillery was built in 1806 [41].

Efficient mills were needed for threshing the grain for malting, and William Young took on the lease of Craigencalt Mill and lands from Raith Estates (William Ferguson) sometime after 1790. The exact date for this lease starting is not known and neither is it known exactly when the new mill was built. Sometime between 1790 and 1810, the new mill at Craigencalt was built by William Ferguson and tenants John Ewan and William Fair [32]. There is some evidence that John Ewan was associated with the Young family but this is not by any means conclusive. However, William Young soon acquired the lease and it is clear from later records (see below) that the Youngs owned all the machinery rather than leased it, strongly suggesting a connection of both men together to the building or at least the commissioning of the mill. The mill contained large modern threshing machinery which would make an efficient and economic contribution to the whisky making process. A new mill pond, situated directly above the new mill was constructed to replace the old mill pond of Damhead and a mill cottage built to provide maintenance on site. All this would account for Robert Young's claim to the Philp Trust in 1857 [42] that he intended to take roans, roofs, stone troughs, feeding byres and threshing machinery if the Trust did not want to purchase them from him. The Trust refused any purchase but replied by saying that "*the heaviest item is the mill which invariably belongs to the tenant and this will be sold to the incoming tenant or disposed of*" at the end of the lease. The minutes go on to comment that the mill was in good condition and improvements may be made at the time of the new tenant. Robert Young was in his 80th year and not likely to renew his lease when it was due in 1863. There are hardly any references to the mill in the Philp Trust minutes and all the maintenance appears to be done by the tenant with no financial contribution from the landlord. One thing that can be concluded is that Craigencalt and the Grange Distillery in Burntisland, were closely linked for many years.

Grange Distillery had one of the highest productions of whisky in Scotland. From 1820 to 1821 it processed 15,853 gals of spirit, 3,520 bushels of malt and 2,100 bushels of raw grain. In 1836 William Young & Co, Grange, malted 13,740 bushels of barley and used 18,858 bushels of grain [45].

So what happened to the old mill? In a letter from Mr Young to the Philp Trust in 1850 he requested money for repairs to the old mill which it said had long been used as a cot house (£21:14/9d). The Philp Trust responded that repairs were to be at the tenants expense [43] which was not the normal situation.

William Young and both of his sons, half brothers, Robert (1777-1860) and William (jnr)(1786-1855), were involved at Craigencalt, Robert more so towards brother William's death. Robert held the lease for the last five years until his death at the age of 83.

Between them, these three men held the tenancy of Craigencalt Mill and lands for over half a century. All the changes and improvements to the property and land at this time were overseen by them, They often took decisions to do things before having the Trust's agreement and often they had to accept doing the work at their own cost. Unlike most tenant farmers they were not hindered by the usual financial constraints. This evidently caused significant friction with the trustees of the Philp Trust.

The following information on the Youngs is taken from Kirkton Old Church Conservation Project [44].

William Young (1745-1831) (father)
William was born at Hattonburn House in Orwell Parish, Milnathort, Kinross. He had six children with his first wife Margaret Gulland including Robert before she died. He married his second wife Helen Simson (or St Clair) and moved to Burntisland where he had a further four children including William.

Robert Young (1777-1860)

Robert's mother was Margaret Gulland , his father's first wife. He was born at Hattonburn, Orwell and moved to Burntisland when he was 9 years old. He went into his father's business and would have been very involved in the building of the new distillery. He did not marry in his youth but built Colinswell House for himself. Gradually he purchased several local properties,Gedsmill. Craigholm, Binnend, Whinnyhall, Common, Rodanbraes, Kinghorn Loch, Lochlands, a small part of Craigencalt, and Gallahill [Gallowhill]. In the 1851 census he was down as a landed proprietor of 300 acres. In 1849, he married Ann Chalmers who was much younger than him and together they had 3 children.

William Young (1786-1855)

William was born at Grange House in Burntisland on the 2nd Oct 1786. He married Mary Purvis (1796-1857)[42] and they had six children. Two of his sons died before him - eldest William died in 1854 aged 33, and John was killed in an accident aged 26. Joseph moved to Folkestone for health reasons and died in 1864 aged 41. Joseph and another son Thomas (merchant in Leith) became very rich. Daughters Helen and Elizabeth remained single, living in Burntisland. William lived at Newbigging with his family then moved to Grange House where he died in 1855, aged 69.

A typical 18th century threshing machine driven by a water wheel. Threshing required much power and a barn - before the days of combined harvesters [46]

Craigencalt Farm was moved from near Grange Farm to the mill in 1891, when a gentleman's residence was needed for the tenant farmer.

The corn mill that existed in 1682, showing the exterior wall that held the waterwheel and the corresponding interior wall. The lower part of the wheel wall has been reconstructed. The survey of 1682 had reported this wall to be in a very poor state. Also observe the large doorway with its curved arch. The watercourse ran down the centre of the now farmyard and still exists as a runoff drain.

The water mill with the lade diverted through the new mill pond and down the west side of the new mill around 1790. The pond is shown, as is the sluice housing, from that time. The threshing mill was a much larger building to accommodate the threshing machinery in a barn and storage.

Craigencalt Cottages comprised two cottages in the lower building, built around 1800 probably as a residence and mill office, and two cottages in the upper building built in 1845 for farm workers.

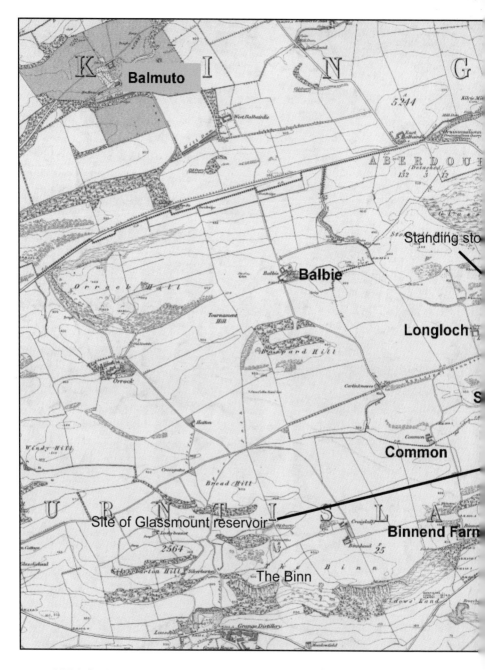

1854 Ordnance Survey Map showing place names circa 1800.

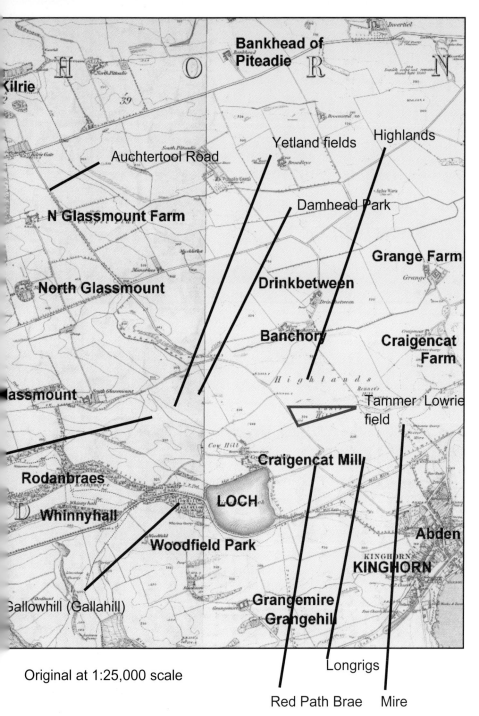

Bankhead of
Piteadie

Kilrie

Yetland fields   Highlands

Auchtertool Road

Damhead Park

N Glassmount Farm

Grange Farm

North Glassmount

Drinkbetween

Banchory

Craigencat
Farm

Glassmount

Tammer Lowrie
field

Craigencat Mill

Rodanbraes

Whinnyhall

Abden

Woodfield Park

KINGHORN

Gallowhill (Gallahill)

Grangemire
Grangehill

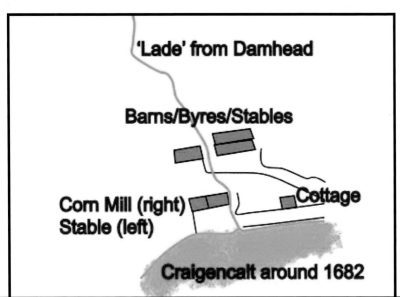

'Lade' from Damhead

Barns/Byres/Stables

Corn Mill (right)
Stable (left)

Cottage

Craigencalt around 1682

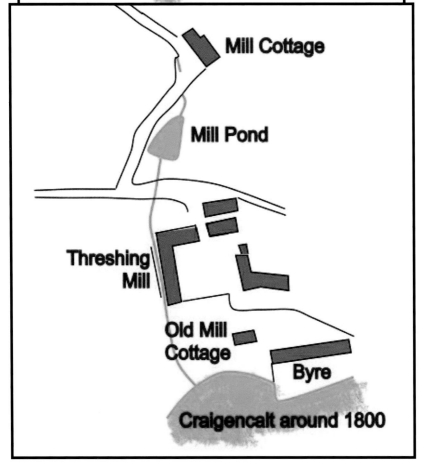

Mill Cottage

Mill Pond

Threshing
Mill

Old Mill
Cottage

Byre

Craigencalt around 1800

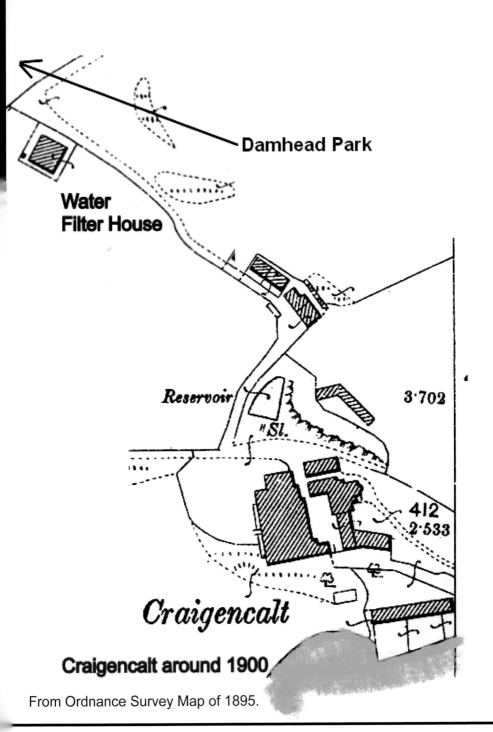

Damhead Park

Water
Filter House

Reservoir

St.

3·702

4I2
2·533

Craigencalt

Craigencalt around 1900

From Ordnance Survey Map of 1895.

8: The Robert Philp Educational Trust takes ownership.

Robert Philp was born in Kirkcaldy on 28th March 1751, the son of William and Alison Philp (Heggie) Robert grew up to be an enterprising business man and travelled over Fife collecting linen from home workers and sold the material at markets like Perth and Dundee. In 1815, with his profit, he bought the West Bridge Mill and bleachfield in Linktown along with some cottages for his workers and a little later a house for himself in Kirkcaldy [47] . The West Bridge Mill has been renovated and is still in use today for housing. In 1824 he purchased Edenhead and Pitlochie and later Lumquhat (Strathmiglo), places of family interest to him [48]. There was a family dispute between brothers John and Robert. John claimed some of Robert's fortune was gained from investments in the West Indies linked to the slave trade. When John changed his family name to Philip, Robert was angry and disowned him. Robert Philp died in 1828 and his wish was for his estate of £70,000 to be used to set up a Trust for "the education and clothing of poor children" and the money not go to his relatives. Robert Philp's tombstone, in the Old Parish Church graveyard in Kirkcaldy, gives details on how his money was to be invested. The Philp family did contest his will but a decree in favour of the Trust was decided [49]. Philp schools were set up by the Trust for children in Kirkcaldy, Linktown, Pathhead and Kinghorn and were up and running within 5 years of his death [50].

In his will, Robert Philp set out clear wishes of how the Trust should be set up and operate. He instructed that the spinning mill and bleaching field in Linktown was be sold and the capital invested. The interest from this was to be used to provide education for poor children. Money was allowed for teachers, books and clothing, Christian education and Sunday evening school. He put huge detail into his will stating his aim for children was "to excite in them a spirit of education". The first governors of the Trust were Simon Dempster, George Aitkin and Douglas Morrison who were merchants in Kirkcaldy, James and

Alexander Bogie who were manufacturers; the men were probably business friends of Robert Philp. At the first meeting of the Philp Trust on 18th April 1828, the title deeds listed included Edenhead, Pitlochie and Lumquhat but no other farms [51].

To put things into context, Robert Philp lived at the same time as some great Scottish names, like Robert Owen of New Lanark, Robbie Burns and Adam Smith. The industrial revolution was in full flow and Adam Smith, another son of Kirkcaldy, had not long published his book "The Wealth of Nations". Life was changing for many ordinary families, with towns booming in population and needing to be fed. Robert Philp's philanthropist idea of providing schools for the poor was not an unknown thing to do at this time but it was far reaching. Funding to pay for schools had to come from an investment, and the purchase and management of farms was the investment agreed upon by the Philp Trust.

Whinnyhall came up for sale in 1825 after the owner, Mr W. Wemyss died at Cuttlehill in Aberdour. There was a sale by auction of Whinnyhall, Roddenbraes (feu to the crown), Binnend and Common (feu to the town of Kinghorn) consisting of 243 acres and 21 acres in hard wood [52]. Mr Wemyss held all the land except Gallowhill, loch and lochlands leased by the town of Kinghorn [53]. A detailed plan of the estate of Whinnyhall was made by William Crawford of Edinburgh in 1827 [54]. The estate was purchased by Robert Young. Thomas Stocks rented Whinnyhall from 1835 to 1859 [53]. There are letters of William Moyes (together with David Moffat) on sequestration of land and crops at Lochlands for collection of debts at the time of sale. [55].

Banchory and Chesters farms are advertised for sale in 1829 [56]; possibly Drinkbetween was included, and in 1830 Craigencalt is advertised in the Edinburgh Gazette [57]. The Philp Trust purchased these farms from Robert Ferguson of Raith. In the account of charge and discharge, Banchory was purchased for £8,900 and Drinkbetween and Craigencalt Mill for £29,000 [59]. The minutes of the Philp Trust were detailed and informative and give a great insight into the running of the farms. Committees met regularly to decide on actions for repairs and improvements and the Trust remained closely involved.

Robert Meldrum was the tenant in Banchory when the Philp Trust took over and he continued to the end of his lease, paying £340/annum [60]. He was often in arrears with his payments and asked for reductions [61,62]. It was agreed to put a second storey on the farm house (Grieves House) and to erect cottages for 2 families and to repair the stable at Banchory [60]. William Young was the tenant at Craigencalt. He was concerned about the loch dyke and a meeting ensued with him, the Philp Trust and Mr Green from the Town Council. It was agreed to build a wall on the water's edge and to leave gaps where the cattle could drink and to have stone covers fitted [63]. In 1833 Craigencalt had the expense of new fences and gates between parks (fields) and for making a cattle yard. The Trust agreed to pay [64]. The 1830s seem to have been a time of decline of grain prices and tenants finding it harder to manage. Thomas Laurie (otherwise Lowrie and lessee of Tammer Lowrie field) and Alex Galloway, two tenants of tofts (cottages) at Damhead asked for a reduction in their rent from £48 to £40 [64]. Both are still tenants in 1837 [65,66]. Craigencalt Mill asked for a reduction in its annual lease and so did William Lesslie, the tenant of Drinkbetween. Both were given a reduction of £50 [67] and a wooden potato house for £33 built at Drinkbetween [68]. Robert Meldrum of Banchory continued to be in arrears with his rent and in 1842 the Governors agreed to sequestration but a deal was reached instead.

There are quite a few improvements and repairs at Craigencalt during the first 10 years of the Philp Trust. In 1833 a sketch for improvements to Damhead Park and 22 acres of Craigencalt Mill was made, and to reclaim and improve 7 acres of land. The expense was to be shared with the tenant [62]. In 1836 the stable wall and roof at the mill needed repair at a cost of £19 [69]. In 1837 there was flooding at Craigencalt from Damhead Park and Mr Young offered to take it over and improve drainage for £30 [70]. In 1842 Robert Young put forward a plan, specification and estimate of costs of repairs and improvements needed at Craigencalt Mill. James Aitkin of Tyrie approved the recommendations for the Governors at a cost of £340..16/- and this was agreed. The erection of a dwelling house would have cost £550 and this did not go ahead. [71] William and Robert Young (the present tenants) had substantial homes of their own in Burntisland, living at Grange House and Collinswell House respectively, so it was not necessary to live at Craigencalt. On 30th May 1839 a livestock sale was advertised in the Caledonian Mercury newspaper at Craigencalt Mill Farm [72]. This indicates that the land was used for both crops and pasture. Farming was growing in wealth during this time and money was available for alterations and upgrades to buildings as well as providing funds for the running of the Philp Schools by the Trust.

In 1843 a new let was advertised for Craigencalt Mill and also for the Acre Lands occupied by Andrew Robertson and Thomas Stocks. Leases were set for 19 years and the previous leases had been granted in 1824 before the Philp Trust took over. The leases were renewed to the same tenants [72]. Thomas Stocks also had a year on year lease of Highland Acres [73]. Andrew Robertson took over the lease of Banchory Farm from the late Robert Meldrum [73]. Banchory at this time has 200 acres and employed 16 labourers [74]. William Young undertook a lot of improvements at Craigencalt; in 1844 he put in a report of all the work that he had undertaken; without the prior approval of the Trustees. He had covered in the water course from Damhead down to the steading, the sides of the drain being built with stone and lime of the best mason work and the top laid with strong slabs [75]. This stream can be seen just at the corner of Craigencalt Cottages before it goes beneath the track and down to the mill pond. This gave extra pasture in Cow Hill. The stable was mended. He added a cart shed. He made a plea for

Lade (Loch Burn) enclosed in 1844 at Craigencalt Cottage

better accommodation for his farm labourers, describing their dwellings as miserable hovels in danger of falling down. He unilaterally decided to demolish the tofts at Damhead and he had to re house the families at Dodhead, some distance away, near Burntisland. He asked for a couple of new cottages to be built on site by the following summer. The total cost of his works came to £144 and the Trust agreed to pay £60 of the cost [73]. William Hunter was employed to build two cot houses and a cart shed for the cost of £162, half the cost coming from the teins of 1844 and half from 1845 [76]. The cost went over budget, with extra masonry work added from Milne and Gow, and more drainage put in by Thomas Braid but these costs were declined by the Trust [77]. The two new cot houses referred to were situated alongside two existing cot houses at the present Craigencalt Cottages. In 1990 glass was unearthed at the older cottages and was dated to around 1830 by Historic Scotland. It is thought to have come from a roof light in either a thatch, turf or corrugated iron roof. The pantile roof was probably put in at a later date. A date for when the first two cottages were built remains unknown although it is probable that they were built with the new mill (1790-1800) and part of one of them contained an office. The area around and to the rear of the cottages is known as the cot field on a crop map of 1853 [79].

Considerable improvements in the drainage of fields were made at this time. Mr Young and Mr Robertson agreed to drain water from Craigencalt land at Longrigs. The drain cut was 32 chains long and drained a considerable part of Craigencalt Farm [76]. Mr Young also applied to improve 3 scots acres of waste ground and to enclose the servants garden at a cost of £110 and the Trust paid 50% [62]. Mr Young proposed to improve his Highland drainage by trenching it and taking good earth from low ground for infill. He wanted to remove boulders and put in small stone for better drainage too [80]. The Statistical Account of 1840 [81] reports that there was good investment in improvements in drainage and trenching in agricultural land at Kinghorn. Cattle were mainly of native breed although some foreign breeds were brought in from other countries for fattening and these could fetch good prices. Cheviot and black face cross sheep were also kept [81].

Improvements continued at Craigencalt. In 1848, Mr Young wanted to build more stabling as a horse was killed by another because the stable was too small and lacked dividers. The Trust agreed to an estimated cost of £40 [82] and to the addition of a new byre for £19 [83]. In 1850 Mr

Young presented statements to the Trust for building a water tank, stone troughs in-feeding byres and for drainage repairs to cot houses but payment was declined [84]. Later he wrote to request a liquid tank, estimated £40 and repairs to the old mill which had long been used as a cot house. The tank was agreed but repairs to the cot house were to be at the tenants expense [43]. In 1852 Mr Young wanted a straw house at the upper part of the threshing barn, a cattle court and hen house for £40. If the Youngs had asked before they acted it may have been that the Trust would have been more co-operative as they were much more generous and sympathetic to their other tenants. On the other hand the Youngs may have considered the necessity to ask as an irritation!

In 1854, The Fife and Kinross Name Book Vol.135 gave descriptions of many places in the area, Craigencalt was said to be a large farmstead where the farm servants and stewards of the proprietor lived. There was a mill here, and Cowhill was mentioned as a small green hill to the north of the mill. Robert Young had the lease for Craigencalt and he lived at Collingswell, Burntisland. Mr Young's brother lived at Grange House, west of the distillery and near the row of cottages called Dodhead. At Whinnyhall there was a new gentleman's house, a good farmhouse with offices and the farm had long strips of plantations and evergreens. North Glassmount House was described as a good house with a farmstead and gardens. It was the summer residence of Dr Wilson who lived in London, the furniture of this house was advertised for sale in 1855 [85]. There is a steading to the North also called North Glassmount and Longloch was a farm steading occupied by farm servants. Rodanbraes was a row of cottages occupied by farm servants. Mr R S Burridge lived at Grangehill farmhouse and Woodfield was described as a very poor cottage [86,87].

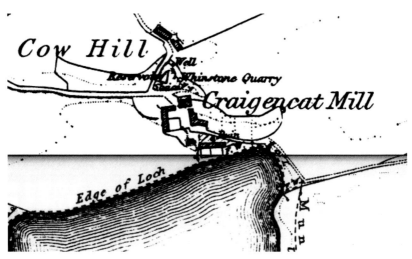

Ordnance Survey plan of 1855. This shows the old mill and new mill.

Robert Young corresponded with the Philp Trust after his brother's death in 1855. He asked for payment for improvements to cot houses but this was refused [89]. In September 1856 Robert Young claimed monies from the Trust for repairs and improvements to the farm and the repair to three cot houses. Mr Young then had part of one of the cottages at Craigencalt Cottages lathe and plastered without permission and was again refused payment. The occupants of the other two cottages complained of damp due to being built on an excavated site with the back on a level with roofs, separated by only 7 feet. It is recommended that in the spring the cottages should be inspected and lathed for permanent improvement [42]. This is done by the Trust.

Mr Young' also wanted to enlarge the mill pond to make the running of the mill more efficient but this was rejected by the Trust as this was deemed of no value to the Trust and they claimed the water power to be deficient and an incoming tenant would want to erect a steam engine for threshing [42]. He stated that he intended to take the threshing mill machinery and water wheel at the end of his lease which expired in 1863 [90]. The Trust decided that the discussion to remove items was premature, as the lease had 5 years to run. The Trust said they would not buy these items, which belonged to the tenant, but as the mill was in a good condition, this would be offered to the next tenant [42].

In January 1857 a report for the Philp Trust on Craigencalt which included Damhead (122 scotch acres) said that it was a good steading, but that no farmhouse existed and would be needed before re-letting. The land was well fenced with stone and lime dykes. The rent in grain was 78 quarters of wheat, barley and oats converted into money [91].

Robert Young died in 1860 and his heir, Robert William was too young to continue the lease so the let of Craigencalt and Damhead Park was advertised in the Fife Herald [92]. The sale of the stock and equipment of Craigencalt was also advertised [93].

There were four offers put in for the new lease, Alex Christie of Balgeddie, Walter Veitch of Grange, Andrew Robertson of Banchory and Alex Lesslie of Drinkbetween. After much discussion, it was decided to accept Mr Robertson's offer as it was desirable to let the farms together. However, Mr Veitch had offered the highest bid and he put in a letter of complaint to the Trustees [94] but to no avail. The new lease of Craigencalt was £200 plus 45 quarters each of wheat, barley and oats in money [95].

With the combining of the farms it is very likely that the water mill was not now needed, as Banchory had a steam driven thresher, and it probably went out of use in 1860.

In 1862, Andrew Robertson wrote to the Trustees to say that he was moving to Cupar and was transferring the lease to his father and brother [96]. In October 1863 there was damage to the stable roof at the steading at Craigencalt and flying debris damaged the roof of one of the cottages and this was repaired [97].

There are no census records for Kinghorn for 1841 as it was lost on a ferry that sank in a storm. The census for 1861 gave an indication of the families living in the farms. Grange Farm had the original Craigencat Farm house close-by and there were cottages linked to it. This causes confusion when looking on census records until the subtle differences of addresses are recognised. Craigencat old farm house had a lower and upper floor and the apartments were named east, west, north and south - all are agricultural workers. Craigencalt Farm situated at Kinghorn Loch had Craigencalt Mill Foremans house where James Clunie, a plowman, and his wife Catherine lived with their five children [31]. James Kulvear and his wife Isobella lived at Craigencalt Mill cottage one [31] and Robert Goodwillie and wife Jane were their neighbours at Craigencalt Mill second cottage (this is thought to be the older dwellings at Craigencalt Cottages [31]). Workers living at the different farms were either recorded as farm labourers or servants in the 1861 census.

In June 1864 William Robertson, who farmed both Banchory and Craigencalt, made a claim of £59.15/- to the Trust for damage to land and byres caused by the overflowing of Kinghorn Loch and this sum for repairs was paid by the Trust 'without prejudice' [98]. The bailiff for the town had raised the level of water in the loch by seven feet, presumably to improve water supply for Kinghorn. Mr Robertson also wrote to say that unless the loch was lowered by 5 foot then more damage would ensue and the march wall would be under water. The lowering of the water level was ordered by the Town Council as someone (unspecified) realised that if they did not do so the embankment at the sluice could collapse, which would cause terrible flooding in Kinghorn. This left the problem of who was responsible for the damage at Craigencalt and the decision for this was left with the courts. The conclusion of the reporter's enquiry was strange but clear. A former resident at Craigencalt, Mrs Gourlay, had confirmed that dykes at the lochside were first built around 1826 and a meeting, between the Philp Trust and the Town Council, to establish land ownerships and responsibilities (after the loch was flooded in 1831) concluded that all land above the normal water line was in private hands and thus flooding by the town was not allowed. The agreement to prohibit flooding was signed by all parties but was never acted upon and, within two years of the meeting, a set of byres and a shed had been erected on land which was known could flood if the loch overflowed again. Thus the tenant (of the Philp Trust) had built or used the property in the knowledge of it flooding [99]. The Old Mill cottage was therefore abandoned. This did not stop the doubtful actions of the bailiff and in 1882 there was damage to the road by the flooding of Kinghorn Loch too [100].

In 1866 a new lease was given to William Robertson for an annual rent of £421:8s 9d [101]. The Earl of Leven offered £428 to abolish an historical stipend payment to the Trust which he had been bound to since passing over the forsaid lands. This was approved by the court [102]. In 1871 Banchory and Craigencalt extended to 350 imperial acres with cottage accommodation for 12 families [103].

The 1871 Census returns [104] showed that some working families had moved farms within the area. This was a common occurrence depending on who they found themselves working for each year. The Greig family, Robert (40) and wife Eliza (33) lived at Craigencalt Mill Cottage. They had 4 children, the eldest is 14 and William (plowman) and Mary Grieve lived at the second Craigencalt Mill Cottage with 3 children. Ann Smeaton also lived at Craigencalt Mill Cottage with her daughters and mother Rachel Coventry who is 90. All are registered as agricultural workers. The Clark, Aitken, Keddie and Iron families all resided at Banchory Cottages. There were a large number of families in the 1871 census, all working in farming in the surrounding area at that time.

In 1872, an inspection of Craigencalt Cottages by Mr Waddell, a Burntisland builder, Mr Anderson, a wright and Mr Muir, a slater, reported on improvements that were required. They recommend that earth floors be replaced with wood, repairs to plaster work, a complete overall of roofs and rones, with one roof needing to be plastered and lathed and the complete replacement of tiles [105]. In the same year, William Robertson went bankrupt and renounced his lease [106]. The lease was advertised. Tom Laurie also gave up his small possession of the Highlands lease [107] to add this land to the title. A new lease for Banchory and Craigencalt Farms was offered to George Davidson of Auchtertool for £1100 [108]. £25 was allowed for work on the cottages at Craigencalt. The farming years were becoming more difficult at this time and profits greatly reduced.

By 1879 farming was in a depressed state and several of the Philp Trust farms were in arrears with payments. George Davidson and Alexander Lesslie, along with others, requested a reduction in rent, and a 10% reduction was agreed [109]. A fall in prices and poor returns continued into the eighties and the Philp Trust proposed to invest in better returns than the farms [110] so railway stock was considered if farms were sold. In 1883 George Davidson accepted giving up the lease of Banchory and Craigencalt [111]. A new lease gave the option for a tenant to have a farmhouse built at Craigencalt for an additional annual rent of £30 [112]. No suitable offers came forward so it was decided to continue with Mr Davidson until the lease ended in 1891 [113]. By 1885 the arrears in rent on the three farms of Craigencalt, Banchory and Drinkbetween were written off by the Philp Trust.

In the 1881 Census records [114] there are lots of families who lived and worked on the farms in the area. Robert and Jessie Coutts still lived at Kilrie House, where he was the coachman. Two of their offspring had progressed well through education. Son, Robert was a Bank Accountant in Annan, Dumfriesshire and daughter Jessie was an infant school teacher [114]. Others like the Gillespie family were still working and living in cottages at Long Loch farm [114]. The Watson family, living in Banchory Old Farm House in 1881, seemed to move around a lot and were recorded living in different places within the locality with each census [114]. This all depended on who hired them for work each year, living was transient and packing up belongings in a cart and moving was common for many folk. George Davidson lived at Banchory Farm House farming 350 acres and employing 11 men 8 women and 2 boys and 2 living in servants[114]. Alexander and Jane Lesslie lived at the newly built Drinkbetween farm house and he was now 63 and has 139 working acres with 4 men, 5 women and 2 boys assisting him. There was no farm house at Craigencalt Mill, only cottages for workers. The tenant at Craigencalt, George Davidson, was also the tenant of Banchory where he was resident, so did not require accommodation elsewhere. James Aitken and family was recorded as living at Craigencalt Mill Farmhouse, probably converted from one of the mill buildings [114]. John Lawson and family lived at Craigencalt Mill Cottage, all working as farm labourers [114].

On 17th July 1873 there is a wonderful description of a wedding at Kilrie [115] of the daughter of John Drysdale, the farmer, to Robert Tullis. The event is described in the Fife Herald. The celebration involves all the workers from surrounding farms. Robert Coutts, the coachman presided over the evening. Kilrie has been the home of the Drysdales for over 200 years.

A Scottish wedding in 1780.

MARRIAGE REJOICINGS AT KILRIE

Tuesday last was a day to be remembered by the quiet and undemonstrative residenters in and around the district of Kilrie. The occasion was the marriage of the eldest daughter of John Drysdale, Esq. of Kilrie, to Robert Tullis, Esq., Rothes. The interesting ceremony was performed by the Rev. Mr Reid, Kettle, and after the usual greetings, the young couple departed on their marriage tour amid a storm of old boots and shoes. In the evening the tenantry, the male and female servants on the estate, and the ploughmen with their wives and families on the several farms belonging to Kilrie, viz., Kilrie, Piteadie, Glassmount, Langloch, Balbeardie, Binend, Commin, and Whinnyhall, were entertained to supper at Kilrie farm. For the few previous days preparations had been making on a large scale for the event. Flagstaffs were reared at several vantage points, and triumphal arches, done up with flowers and evergreens, were thrown across gateways, while partners for the dance had been bespoke, and gay dresses provided for the occasion; so that when the time arrived quite a galaxy of youth and beauty came forth from cottage and cotter houses, and, busked in their best, tripped along by hedge rows to the rendezvous. About eight o'clock the company, which numbered about 160, sat down to supper in the granary, which was fitted up for the occasion in a very artistic fashion. A long extemporised table stretched the whole length of the building, and may be said to have actually groaned under the weight of the many good things deposited on it. Amongst the ornaments with which it was adorned were several cups gained by Mr William Drysdale for prize cattle. Overhead, and covering the naked beams, were festoons and garlands of evergreens and flowers, whilst lamps were suspended from the green boughs, and reflected their light on the many-coloured dresses of the fair wearers sitting around. Mr Robert Coutts, coachman, presided, and Mr James Davie having asked the blessing, the company entered at once upon their sumptuous repast, when plates were emptied with a speed truly astonishing. About half-past nine a number of the ladies and gentlemen who were guests at Kilrie House came over and honoured the company with their presence. Mr William Drysdale took the chair,

9: Water Supply for Kinghorn

The water supply for Kinghorn had always been linked to the loch that lies above the town. The loch had supplied both water for domestic use and industrial purposes for flax mills that flourished in Kinghorn. With streams running into the loch the water was never stagnant and there was usually an adequate supply. The people of Kinghorn still have the right to use the water in the loch. As public health became more important in the 19th century, Kinghorn Town Council looked many times at how the water supply could be improved. In 1874 a meeting took place at Craigencalt between the Provost and Magistrates of Kinghorn and the Philp Trust to agree to putting in a clearwater tank and to pipe water from the Craigencalt Burn to Kinghorn. The Governors were happy to consider this [116] and later the work was done. Soon, problems with the booming Burntisland Oil Shale Works [117] added pressure and urgency to ensure a good water supply to Kinghorn. Different options were investigated by the Town Council and in 1888 they decided to abandon the idea of a waterworks above Craigencalt Mill and to build a works with a clear water tank and enclosed filters to treat the water at a reservoir at Common [118]. This plan did not come to fruition and in 1892 a meeting took place between the Trust and the Police Commission for Kinghorn to ask to construct the reservoir on Craigencalt land and pay compensation to the tenant. A sale of 2.5 acres of land to make Glassmount reservoir was finalised on 7th January 1893 [119] and permission agreed to take clay by contract for the construction. A pathway down the side of the field from the reservoir to the filter beds was made, and new treatment works installed at Craigencalt. Later in 1930 an Unemployment Grant Committee [120] gave £3,600 to Kinghorn Council for construction of new filter beds to give employment to those out of work in the depression time.

This system for the water supply for Kinghorn remained in place until water was supplied from Castlehill Reservoir at Glendevon. In 1999 a new bigger water tank was built at Craigencalt, as a service reservoir to complete the upgrade. The old Glassmount Reservoir was decommissioned in the 1980s.

10: Changing Times

In 1882 the Educational Endowment (Scotland) Act oversaw the gradual transfer of schools to Board Schools. The endowment fund, created from the Philp Trust that had been permanently investing in land estates had provided income to run the Philp Schools. The creation of state run Board Schools meant that times were changing [110] and heralded the gradual run down of Philp Trust school provision and dis-investment in the farms through their sale but over a period of some thirty years.

Mr Davidson renounced his lease from Martinmus 1890 with a further reduction of rent so that he did not finish in arrears [124] and Mr Lesslie of Drinkbetween agreed to take on the lease of Banchory [125]. He had several demands for Banchory and finds the house in need of decorating [126]. The work is carried out though Mr Lesslie is repeatedly asked to pay 5% towards cattle courts and fencing [131]. The lease of Craigencalt is given to John Craig formally of Argyle for £335 [127]. Mr Craig put in a request for additions to the steading and a dwelling house and William Little, architect was asked to draw up the plans for all the work [128]. Work proceeded well on the farm house which was built in 1891, eventually coming in at £2,301, over budget by £82 [129]. The address given by Mr Craig was Woodfield, Craiges Cult Farm in the 1891 census [139]. He was living there with wife, Margaret and five adult offspring, all working at the farm. In 1893 Mr Craig built a road to his house from the public road, and an entrance to his house from the farm steading [130]. During his tenancy, meetings took place with the Police Commissioners for Kinghorn to discuss constructing a reservoir on Craigencalt land for the water supply for Kinghorn. This was agreed and the tenant paid compensation [131]. On 25th July 1892 the deal for the reservoir was signed [132]. and the land sold to the Police Commission [133]. Land was also given for a footpath to go between the reservoir [134] and filters and water from the new pipes were to go to Craigencalt and Banchory [130]. Mr Craig was due £183 in compensation for land lost to Kinghorn Commissioners [135].

Mr Robert Kirke, living in London, wrote to the Trust offering £12/annum for shooting rights on the land of Craigencalt, Banchory and Drinkbetween [137]. The three tenants were aggrieved that the profit from the shooting arrangement would all go to the Trust and following on from their complaint they were allowed half of the rent. Mr Kirke would be fully responsible for any damage claimed by the tenants [138].

Margaret Craig died and John married Annie Douglas of Oban, but John Craig also died, aged 61 years, in 1900 [139]. Mr Craig was in arrears with rent and the Trust decided that Craigencalt would be re-let at Martinmus [139]. On petition from the residents, the condition of the cottages at Craigencalt had been inspected by Dr Naismith, the sanitary inspector in 1899 and found to be in a bad state. Under the terms of the lease the tenant was responsible for the repairs [141] and repairs were done. New pig sties were put in along the back wall [142] by the Trust.

In 1900 a new tenant came to Craigencalt; a William Young of Skerrington Mains Farm, Lanarkshire, who was no relation to the Young family who owned the distillery in Burntisland and who held the tenancy of Craigencalt throughout the first part of the nineteenth century. He made an offer of £375 for the lease, in excess of the £300 offered from Mr William Lesslie (son of Alexander)[143] of Drinkbetween. Mr Young asked for conditions of his acceptance. These were several fences to be erected along boundaries of land and roadside, sliding doors to be put in at the lochside cattle court, and various gates and troughs to be added. These demands were all agreed by the Trust [144]. Fence costs were 1/6 per yard [145]. There was an auction of all the stock, farm implements and horses for sale from Craigencalt and Mr Young was the main buyer, the horses sold for £120 and the pony for £28 [146]. In December 1900 an inspection of the property at Craigencalt was made and some serious repairs found to be needed. The barn roof needed lath and plastering and tiles replacing. The entire outside of the steading woodwork needed painting and a re-routing of the drain through the steading put into a built culvert [147]. The cottages at Craigencalt were again found to be in a poor state and required rones (guttering) to be put at the back of them [147], new window frames and the replacement of one floor. Painting and papering was needed throughout the cottages [147].

There was a disastrous harvest in 1903 and Mr Young, and Mr Lesslie, Banchory and Drinkbetween asked for a reduction in their rent for that year but the Trust declined [148]. Mr Young reported that the wall along the lochside, at the cattle courts, was in a poor condition and flooded in winter. It is agreed for the wall to be heightened and continued around the west end of the cattle court and it was agreed to erect three buttresses for support [149]. The Trust minutes stop in 1906 (although the Trust continued until 1919). No further entries were made about work to the farms of Banchory, Drinkbetween and Craigencalt which the Trust still owned [150] although the East Fife farms had been sold by this time.

Robert Young, takes Craigencalt tenancy in 1900 at age of 28 and here for more than 50 years.

William Young and his wife Jane brought a long period of stability to Craigencalt Farm which they purchased from the Philp Trust in November 1919. They were a well liked couple who involved themselves with the local community. In 1904 Mr Young was elected to Kinghorn Parish Council on which he served for many years [151]. He served on several committees and became chairman of the Public School Board [152]. He was elected to the Fife Agricultural Society and was a well known enthusiast for breeding his favourite Friesian cattle [153]. He won competitions for his prize winning bull Douneside Pilot and offspring, Douneside Knight. He had remarkable success with his Friesian cow Violet, who was champion for the best milk yield 2 years running [393,394]. Sadly in 1939, one of his cattlemen, Andrew Kinninmonth was killed by a bull, highlighting that farming can be a dangerous business [156].

William Young was presented with the Royal Humane Society's Certificate for trying to rescue 3 boys from Kinghorn Loch on 10th February 1917. He was commended for his brave action [157]. *The story is recounted in a later section.*

William Young sold Craigencalt Farm in 1953 and there was an auction sale of all his stock, crops and farm implements [158]. The farm was bought by Mr and Mrs Alston, but they did not stay long [159]. It was then purchased by the Cochran family of Banchory Farm who have now farmed in the area for many years.

Old maps show that the type of farming, a mixture of arable and pasture has changed little over the centuries. The number of people working in farming has reduced greatly with high tech machinery and much greater capacity to work the fields much more efficiently. Craigencalt and Kinghorn Loch is now more a place for recreation, with water sports of canoeing and sailing, leisure activities like bird watching and walking taking prominence, but there is still plenty of good farming too.

The agricultural mill had been situated at Craigencalt since before 1583 right through to 1860 and the buildings still exist and set to interest visitors for many years to come.

11: Banchory and Drinkbetween Farms

The three farms of Craigencalt, Banchory and Drinkbetween have been closely connected for a long time. The Philp Trust purchased and managed them through its Farming Committee for almost a century. The lands of Banchory and Drinkbetween were purchased from Robert Ferguson of Raith Estate by the Philp Trust in 1832 [59]. Together with Craigencalt, the investment provided the income for running the Philp Schools as instructed in the Will of Robert Philp. William Lesslie became the tenant for Drinkbetween and he complained that the rent was too high and it was reduced by £50 [67]. Robert Meldrum continued his lease for Banchory and it was agreed to put a second storey on the farmhouse (Grieves house) and to erect cot houses for two families and repair the stable. He was also in arrears on his rent and obtained a reduction [61]. The problem continued and the Trust called a meeting. Eventually, in 1842 the Governors reached a deal with Mr Meldrum.

Andrew Robertson who had the let of Kinghorn Acres and Mireside, which he proposed to drain, took over the lease of Banchory in 1847 after the death of Robert Meldrum. The Lochacres were added to the Banchory lease [167,168]. A committee visit to Banchory in 1849 revealed several improvements and repairs were needed. The stable needed to be made bigger to take 10 horses, the cattle shed made larger, a new granary barn and cart shed erected and a new farm house needed. The dwelling house needed to be made water tight and urgent roof repairs done [169]. All was made good at the Trust's expense [170]. It was also agreed to build two new cot houses at Banchory [171]. The 1851 census, had Andrew Robertson, who is 56, and his wife Isabella living at Banchory Farm and tending 187 acres with their sons John (22) and Andrew(17) and three living in employees [172]. More improvements were made in 1852 with building a straw storage house, boiling shed, turnip shed and a wall for the cattle court. The estimated cost of £540 was agreed [173]. Banchory had a steam threshing mill installed and alterations were made at Damhead to provide the water supply to it [174]. The cattle court was enlarged and it was found that urine from cattle ran down behind the farm house causing the walls to become damp. It was decided to build a new house on the west side of the stack yard [175]. The cost of the new house was not to exceed £600 [176]. In 1856 Mr Robertson reported that the house was nearly finished, and needed rough casting. William Innes did the work [177]. The house had a walled garden and wall at the front done by William Bathron [178]. The final cost of the house which was described as first rate was £626..2/6 [91].

There was an interesting and long saga about a road which is first agreed by Mr Robertson of Banchory and Mr Drysdale of Kilrie in 1855. The new road was made from Glassmount to South Glassmount and turned to run east along the march lands of Damhead and Craigencalt through to the Auchtertool Road. The road worked well to serve both farmers but Lord Rosslyn and Mr Ferguson, the land owners did not want to pay towards road costs or fencing. The result was they had gates locked on the road, preventing entry. Mr Robertson got so upset about this that he broke down the gates and a solicitors letter was sent to the Trust shutting off the road [121]. The problem erupts once more, 30 years later when a summons was issued by Lord Rosslyn's agent against Mr Davidson (the new tenant) and the Philp Trust preventing them from using the 'Craigencalt Road' [122]. The disputed road started and finished on Lord Rosslyn's land but otherwise was on Banchory's land. The dispute went to informal arbitration, and a Mr Oswald of Dunniker gave award against the Governors of the Trust for Lord Rosslyn, and this was accepted [123]. South Glassmount owners have the right to access this road in perpetuity. Finally Lord Rosslyn was offered £20 for use of the road by Mr Davidson for the remainder of his lease and this was agreed.

In the Census of 1861 Mr Robertson was farming 389 acres and employing 12 men, 2 boys and 4 servants at Banchory[31]. His son Andrew was living with him and later in the year he married Eliza Cochrane of Glasgow [181]. Andrew moved to Cupar and left the lease with his father and brother William [96]. In 1866 William Robertson renewed the lease for Banchory at £609 and Craigencalt at £421 [101]. There was a depression in farming by the 1870's and William Robertson gave up Banchory and Craigencalt and his crops went up for sale [182]. George Davidson of Auchtertool took over the lease of both farms for a rent of £1100/annum [183]. Mr Davidson wanted to take down the working horse stables and to add to the riding stables, more reeds (cattle), and a new turnip shed. Some of the improvements go ahead. In the 1881 Census, George Davidson was living in Banchory with his sister Jessie. He employs 11 men, 8 women and 2 boys and 2 servants. Mr Davidson gave up the leases on Banchory and Craigencalt at Martinmus 1883 and they were advertised but he puts in an offer a little higher than John Robertson, Andrew Robertson's son, and was accepted again by the Trust [113]. His arrears were written off [184]. Mr Davidson struggled with payment of rent until he finally gave up his tenancy in 1890 [185]. Later he married Rachel and they had 3 children, Thomas, Eliza and Jessie. Mr Davidson left Banchory to live at Kirkbank Road in Burntisland and by 1901 was living in Edinburgh [114].

There was a petition from the workers at Banchory cottages in 1873, for the water pipe from the farm house to be extended, as their only water supply was from the burn which was polluted .[186] The supply was also extended to Drinkbetween house and cottages [187]. The state of farming remains depressed throughout the 1870's and many tenants, including George Davidson and Alexander Lesslie ask for reductions in rents.

Drinkbetween was run down and fields required a lot of drainage. Mr Robertson helped to supervise this work and the Trust paid half of the cost. [188]. He asked for improvements to Drinkbetween House, Mickleflat cottage repaired, some new dykes and a track to the north fields and also a new water tank and pump [189]. The conclusion was that the dwelling house was to be replaced because it was inferior. Other improvements to byres and steading, and Muckleflat, were also agreed. In 1850 William Little drew up plans for a new house (at a cost not exceeding £350 [84]) and the go ahead given. The old house was converted to a milk house [190]. The new house was built of unmanageable stone gathered from the farm and it has to be rough cast by William Muir at a cost of £4 [191]. A year later, further alterations and repairs were made to pig sties, storeroom, boiling gig, barley houses and stone wall cistern [192]. Mr Lesslie had managed a lot of upgrade in a short period. In 1866 Alexander Lesslie renewed his lease at a rent of £303 annually [101]. There was a down turn in farming over the 70's and all tenants asked for reductions in rents. In the 1881 Census, Alexander

Lesslie was 63 and farming with his wife Jane at Drinkbetween, with 4 men, 5 women and 2 boys working for them [114].

Alexander Lesslie took on the lease of Banchory after Mr Davidson in 1891 [125]. He presented the Trust with a list or repairs needed at Banchory [193]. By 1892 much of the work had been completed [194]. The work cost £402 [129] and he was asked to pay an additional £5 in rent [132]. At this time, Alexander Lesslie, who was getting on in years, asked to assign the lease of both farms to his son, and this was accepted. William Leslie took over the lease and the Trust visited Banchory and Drinkbetween and found them both to be in good order [195]. He asked for a bathroom to be fitted at Banchory farm house, but this was not agreed for 6 years [147]. The estimated cost was £158 [142.] Alexander Lesslie died on the 27th April 1901 and this was a sad occasion for the governors as he had been a tenant with the Trust for such a long time. The Lesslie family kept on the lease until 1919 when Banchory and Drinkbetween were purchased by William Niven of Grangehill Farm [196]. After this it was sold to the Cochran family and remains a well run working farm today. The crops grown are still mainly wheat and barley, with some rape-seed fields. It also has pasture, with similar livestock to a century ago. There is something reassuring about all this.

In the first part of the 19th century, farming grew in prosperity and efficiency and the revenue from the farms gave a good income for the Philp Trust. They were good landowners who kept up repairs and improvements on their farms. There were instances where the Trustees provided a bursary for individual youngsters to attend school when families were faced with hardship. There is a reference in the minutes to John Dunearn, an ostler, who was found drowned in Kinghorn Loch, for his two children to be admitted to the school. Philp Schools, and later the advent of Board Schools equipped rural youngsters to better themselves. There is no indication that farm labourers were suppressed or treated unfairly, though long hours, few holidays and low wages did lead to the formation of the Ploughman's Society locally in 1866. David Smeaton, a ploughman from Banchory Cottages was amongst those who spoke at the Inaugural Meeting in Bridgeton reported in the Fife Herald.

12: Kinghorn and Kinghorn Loch

The town has a long history of its own, connected to the ancient Kings of Scotland, the most famous locally being Alexander III who died close by, setting the inheritance to the Scottish throne in turmoil. In 1611 the Charter of Kinghorn granted the loch and large swaths of land and property to the Burgh of Kinghorn [33] as far west as Common. By 1875 the loch was included in the sale of Whinnyhall estate and remains the property of the Whinnyhall landowners to the present time [197].

For hundreds of years Kinghorn town relied on Kinghorn Loch for its water supply together with a small contribution from Lady Burn which drains the Mire. There were many attempts to persuade the Town Council to raise the level of the loch. In 1796 a petition from the mill owners to raise the level by 3 feet had general support[166] and certainly the level has been raised by this amount. The water flowed out from the loch into the Loch Burn which made its way down through Kinghorn to the sea. Mills interrupted the water flow so that if the wrong measures were taken at the loch, Kinghorn could be flooded. The raising of the sluice wall by 7 feet in 1866 could have resulted in the collapse of the embankment. If someone in authority had not realised the risk and lowered it again, the potential for disastrous damage to Kinghorn may have been realised [99].

After Kinghorn Loch was sold to the Burntisland Oil Company and they set up a Candle Works at the loch, contamination of the water occurred. In 1887 it was reported that pollution of the water had caused hundreds of perch and pike to be killed and washed up on the edge of the loch. The Candle Works were using the loch for cooling purposes [157]. Water samples were taken for analysis and found to contain saline ammonia, albumin and phosphoric acid, and totally unfit for human consumption [198]. After this, the Constabulary for Kinghorn investigated options of bringing water to Kinghorn from Craigencalt and the Philp Trust assisted in this [119,199].

In some very cold winters, Kinghorn Loch freezes over, but the ice is deceptive as the stream flowing into the loch can keep it warmer and the thickness of ice does not build up as in other lochs. Sadly several youngsters have been caught out by a desire to skate and have fun on the ice only to get stranded, or worse, to fall through into the water.

Newspaper reports record these sad events, some with fatalities, such as in 1859 when a group of boys were sliding out on the loch and 3 of them fell through the ice. Two managed to scramble back out but one boy, George Oswald, a joiner's son, drowned [200]. The worst tragedy occurred in February 1917 when farm workers, down at the cattle shed at the lochside, spotted 3 boys walking on the ice. They saw the boys fall through into the icy water and William Young, the farmer at Craigencalt, and his workers rushed to the scene with a rope and ladder. Mr Young crawled on the ladder to the hole and rescued one boy, then went into the water to try and rescue the other two but it was not until the constabulary used a long hook were they able to recover the bodies. The boys, all from Kinghorn were drowned. They were Alexander MacKay (14) William Murphy (13) and Alexander Luciani (11). At the funeral all the folk in Kinghorn lined the High Street as the hearses made their way to the cemetery. It was a very sad day. William Young received a certificate for bravery from the Royal Humane Society for his valiant efforts in trying to save the boys [201].

Not all the incidents result in fatality. During the First World War when thousands of soldiers were resident in Kinghorn and surrounding barracks, defending the Dockyard at Rosyth, a tragedy was averted. In November 1915, three soldiers and their lady companions were on the ice at Kinghorn Loch when it gave way and they fell in. Two soldiers and two ladies got out immediately and they managed to rescue the third soldier. Sgt Major Anderson who was on duty at the former Candle Works, at that time a wartime barracks, then slid a sentry box into the water to pull out Miss Low, of the High Street, Kinghorn. He retrieved her, but the sentry box started to sink so he called to other soldiers to "strip off their puttees" and make a rope so Miss Low, who had lost consciousness was rescued. Once in the warm she recovered [202].

References.

NEWSPAPERS (Reference) then date DD/MM/YYYY:

Caledonian Mercury:				(52)	10/6/1824	(72)	30/5/1839
Dundee Courier:				(4)	25/5/1875	(100)	28/4/1882
(151)	24/11/1904	(152)	10/7/1909	(153)	4/2/1920	(154)	12/2/1927
(156)	24/7/1939	(158)	17/11/1953	(159)	25/12/1953	(196)	10/7/1939
(198)	13/7/1888	(200)	27/2/1893	(202)	23/11/1915		
Dunfermline Press:				(93)	11/10/1860	(181)	21/11/1861
Dunfermline Saturday Press:				(157)	29/10/1887		
Edinburgh Advertiser:				(37)	8/9/1786		
Edinburgh Evening News:				(133)	7/1/1893		
Edinburgh Gazette:				(57)	16/4/1830		
Evening Telegraph:				(120)	9/9/1930	(155)	20/12/1928
(201) 15/5/1917							
Fife Free Press:				(146)	3/11/1900		
Fife Herald:				(92)	9/8/1860	(115)	17/7/1873
(182)	8/8/1872	(183)	3/10/1872	(197)	24/6/1875		
Glasgow Herald:				(118)	18/7/1888	(199)	7/12/1888

NATIONAL ARCHIVE OF SCOTLAND (ref) then NAS catalogue reference:

(7)	GD66/1/2	(9)	GD66/1/49	(11)	GD26/3/221	(16)	GD26/5/631
(17)	GD66/1/122	(18)	GD26/3	(19)	GD26/3/719	(21)	GD26/3/244
(23)	GD26/5/125	(36)	GD26/5/274	(39)	GD76/363	(53)	RHP35987/1-
(54)	RHP3246						

KINGHORN TOWN COUNCIL MINUTES (ref) then date:

(24)	9/11/1730	(160)	19/2/1790	(161)	12/7/1790	(162)	25/9/1790
(163)	4/10/1792	(164)	15/1/1793	(165)	2/10/1793	(166)	22/11/1796

PHILP TRUST FARM COMMITTEE MEETING MINUTES (ref) then date:

(99)	23/1/1866	(101)	1/11/1866	(105)	28/11/1872	(107)	26/7/1872
(109)	29/12/1879	(111)	22/3/1883	(112)	3/4/1883	(126)	18/12/1890
(127)	12/4/1890	(128)	21/3/1891	(129)	24/12/1892	(130)	2/8/1894
(137)	24/11/1894	(138)	12/1/1895	(141)	19/1/1899	(142)	15/9/1899
(143)	29/4/1900	(144)	14/5/1900	(145)	11/6/1900	(147)	26/12/1900

PHILP TRUST GOVERNORS MEETING MINUTES (ref) then date:

(42)	25/3/1857	(43)	30/7/1850	(48)	3/6/1828	(49)	15/1/1829
(50)	1828: Conditions of bequest.			(51)	18/4/1828	(56)	26/10/1829
(59)	27/8/1832 - Account of 1828.			(60)	7/12/1829	(61)	16/10/1833
(62)	9/10/1833	(63)	26/7/1831	(64)	1/7/1833	(65)	26/9/1837
(66)	26/8/1837	(67)	12/8/1831	(68)	12/8/1833	(69)	18/4/1836
(70)	26/9/1837	(71)	15/6/1842	(73)	7/9/1843	(74)	1/6/1843
(75)	3/12/1844	(76)	12/5/1845	(77)	13/1/1846	(80)	10/12/1848
(82)	1/7/1848	(83)	20/8/1847	(84)	7/6/1850	(85)	13/3/1855
(89)	5/3/1856	(90)	24/9/1856	(91)	1857: 1st Annual Report.		
(94)	17/9/1860	(95)	1861: 5th Annual Report			(96)	1/12/1862
(97)	1863: 8th Annual Report.			(98)	1867: 11th Annual Report.		
(102)	20/9/1866	(103)	30/1/1871	(106)	8/7/1872	(108)	13/8/1872
(110)	19/2/1883	(113)	2/7/1883	(116)	9/10/1874	(119)	15/5/1893
(121)	23/5/1855	(122)	22/2/1886	(123)	28/9/1886	(124)	3/10/1887
(125)	13/1/1890	(131)	26/10/1891	(132)	25/7/1892	(134)	24/4/1893
(135)	30/7/1894	(140)	30/10/1899	(148)	25/1/1904	(149)	3/11/1904
(150)	29/1/1906	(167)	26/8/1837	(168)	5/2/1849	(169)	9/10/1849
(170)	1/1/1850	(171)	30/12/1850	(173)	18/6/1852	(174)	22/6/1853
(175)	27/12/1854	(176)	23/5/1855	(177)	16/7/1856	(178)	5/2/1856
(179)	3/12/1860	(184)	26/1/1885	(185)	9/12/1889	(186)	30/6/1873
(187)	26/1/1874	(188)	1/9/1847	(189)	27/7/1848	(190)	4/9/1850
(191)	22/9/1852	(192)	20/6/1853	(193)	24/1/1891	(194)	1/7/1892
(195)	4/10/1894						

(1) "Echline Settlement 8000BC", BBC News, bbc/news/scotland, 18/11/2012

(2) "Joy over Double Stone Age Find in Fife", Scotsman Online, scotsman.com/news, 17/7/2003

(3) "Battle of the Raiths", Nicholson, E.W.B. In Celtic Review VII(25), Feb 1911, p81-88

(5) DD27/3044 Scheduling of Standing Stones, Glassmount, Kinghorn, Fife, 1934, (Historic Environment Scotland)

(6) Register of the Great Seal Vol. 2, 1306-1425

(8) Register of the Great Seal Vol. 3, 1458

(10) "The Scottish Nation - Boswell", electricscotland.com

(13)   Millar, A.H., "Fife: Pictorial and Historical;", A.Westwood & Son, Cupar, 1895

(14)   Reynolds, T.S, "Stronger than a Hundred Men", Johns Hopkins University Press, 198

(15)   A Plan of the Barony of Craigencat, Property of Robert Ferguson', Raith Estate Map 1757

(22)   "Fergusons of Fife, DNA Project"; dna.cfsna.net

(25)   Will of Robert Ferguson of 1781

(26)   "The Berry Papers 1763-1852"; electricscotland.com

(27)   Wikipedia

(28)   MacFarlane Clan & Families Genealogy; clanmacfarlanegenealogy.info

(29)   Historic Environment Scotland - Decisions Portal

(30)   University of St Andrews; http://www-groups.dcs.st-and.ac.uk/history/Biographies/Playfair.html

(31)   1861 Census Records

(32)   Register of Sasine of "Bill of Suspension and Interdict for Kinghorn Town Council, 20 July 1790"

(33)   The First Statistical Accounts of Scotland 1791

(34)   The Elgin Scandal', Geoscientist 04/05/2010

(35)   George IV Reign, Act of Parliament 19-06-1829 Robert Ferguson

(38)   "Lost Distilleries of Scotland"; lostdistilleries.com

(40)   Sequestration of Hattonburn, 1786 (National Archive of Scotland GD76/363 &364, 17

(41)   Burntisland.net

(42)   Kirkton Old Church, Burntisland, Conservation Project: www.kirktonchurch.org.uk

(45)   Section of Reports and Papers of the House of Commons, Vol. 15 1836; "Malting, Brewing and Distillation"

(46)   Brown, J., "Water Power and Watermills", The Crowood Press Ltd., 2011

(47)   "Robert Philp", Kirkcaldy's Famous Folk Vol 1 Kirkcaldy Civic Society

(55)   Letters of William Moyes, (Fife Archive), 1827

(58)   House of Lords, Act of Parliament HL/PO/PB/1/1829/10G4N237, 1829

(79)   Sang Map, 1853 (in National Library of Scotland)

(81)   The Second Statistical Accounts of Scotland, 1840

(86)   Fife & Kinross Name Book Vol. 135, Frasers County Map Sheet 36, 1854

(87)   Fife & Kinross Name Book Vol. 135, 1854